RONDO:

HISTORY & VALUES

2024 EDITION

All inquiries or sales requests should be addressed to:

Planting People Growing Justice Press
P.O. Box 131894
Saint Paul, MN 55113
www.ppgjbooks.com

Printed and bound in the United States of America
First Edition
ISBN: 978-1-959223-54-2

*This activity is supported, in part, by the City of Saint Paul
Cultural Sales Tax Revitalization Program.

SAINT PAUL
S T A R
PROGRAM

TABLE OF CONTENTS

LETTER FROM THE EDITOR

Rondo is our community's story of resilience and power. I had the unique opportunity in 2019 to take the community experience full circle by bringing my Rondo community elders with me for the Year of Return in Ghana. They went along with me to travel through time and space as we reclaimed our place in history.

Being from Rondo means that I know a place called home. I know the importance of having a purpose and walking in faith.

Rondo is my birthright. I was destined to become a freedom fighter. I was inspired by the leadership legacy of Dr. Kwame Nkrumah, the first prime minister of Ghana, to fight for freedom and justice.

Many are unaware that key civil rights leaders gathered in Ghana for a source of inspiration while seeking a roadmap for change. They wanted to understand the power of the Black Star that unites us wherever we are. Dr. Nkrumah shared about this unifying symbol of power when he stated: "I am not African because I was born in Africa but because Africa was born in me."

I give you the invitation today to take a moment to pause and reflect on who you are:

What is your story?

What is your culture and heritage?

"I AM...Rondo and connected to a rich cultural history of unity, faith, and purpose.

I AM...my African roots. I AM...freedom and justice."

Dr. Artika R. Tyner

Editor

Planting People Growing Justice Leadership Institute

HISTORY OF RONDO

The Rondo community has a rich cultural heritage of unity, hope, and faith. During the early to mid-20th century, African Americans made Saint Paul, Minnesota their home. They found refuge in the Rondo community, which is an almost two-square-mile area extending from Rice Street to Lexington Boulevard and from University Avenue to Selby Avenue. Rondo Avenue served as the nexus of community connections with Black businesses, churches, and schools. By the 1960s, eighty percent of African Americans in Saint Paul lived in Rondo.

During the late 1950s, the very existence of Rondo was threatened with the construction of I-94. Nationwide, the Federal Aid Highway Act of 1956 impacted Black communities like Rondo because new highway systems were being built at a rapid pace. Unfortunately, in Rondo, the highway went through the center of the community. This economic hub, which was evidenced by a vibrant Black neighborhood with hundreds of businesses and a self-sustaining Black ecosystem fueled by cooperative economics ("ujamaa"), was destroyed.

The streets of Rondo used to be bustling with shopping, music, and entertainment, and then 300 Black-owned businesses were effectively decimated. The highway also devastatingly eliminated the possibility of any future wealth creation. The hope-filled neighborhood had been filled with beautiful homes that were destined to be inherited by the next generation. With the new highway construction and the exercise of government power to seize private land for public use (eminent domain), Black families lost their homes and the possibility of building wealth. Seven hundred Black-owned homes were demolished. One in eight African Americans lost their homes due to the construction of I-94, which resulted in a $270 million home ownership equity gap in Rondo.

The next chapter of Rondo's history is still being written as a new group of innovators and creatives are organizing for change. Black entrepreneurs are building businesses and serving in the community. Black students are organizing for change. Rondo will continue to rise with renewed hope and soar to new heights due to its fervent commitment to upholding Rondo community values.

Sources:

Minnesota Historical Society Library, https://libguides.mnhs.org/rondo
Reconnect Rondo, https://reconnectrondo.com/
Rondo Past Prosperity Study (2020).

INTRODUCTION

The Core Values of the Rondo Community

The formation of African-American neighborhoods is intricately linked to the history of segregation in the United States, either through formal laws or as a product of social norms and conditions. At the start of the 20th century, this practice of separating African Americans was developed in Rondo. By the 1930s, 87% of African Americans living in St. Paul resided in Rondo and, when this occurred, Rondo became the type of ethnic enclave found in many cities across the United States.

Rondo shared many of the characteristics of other African-American neighborhoods. It was self-contained with an assortment of housing, jobs, churches, social institutions, and community agencies. However, for those looking at Rondo from the outside, opinions were held that described Rondo as a slum or poor urban area in need of repair.

These attitudes were rarely believed by the residents despite the existence of dilapidated houses and pockets of poverty. For the majority, Rondo was "home"—a place representing an authenticity of feeling, passion, and emotions derived from rising above the struggle and suffering of being of African descent in America. It was a place where one could eat the food, tell the stories, praise the Lord, and dance to the music in a dramatic rhythm all our own.

Although the Black population in Rondo was small, a few factors merged to create a situation where the culture of Rondo played a significant role in the development of a vibrant community whose influence spilled beyond the borders of Saint Paul and Minnesota to the nation and the world at large.

Generations of hardship imposed on the African American community forged the development of these attitudes by residents of Rondo. These were the core values of Rondo, and their early introduction and widespread observance gave Rondo a unique flair and confidence to withstand the often-harsh treatment of outer society. The values were:

The goodness of religion; the value of education; the dignity of work; the necessity of social interaction; the importance of economic independence; the majesty of home ownership; the importance of respect for self, family, and others; and the existence of hope.

WORK : Through work, you experience dignity and build your character. African Americans understand that work unleashes one's unique gifts, talents, and abilities; it enables one to earn a living to take care of oneself and one's family. Work defines us, and as descendants we honor our ancestors for their fortitude to survive slavery, never receiving pay for the toil and work that helped build this country. We do the jobs that need to be done, and we do not let others define how we should feel about an honest occupation.

HOME OWNERSHIP : A home is a castle, and owning your home is the ultimate American Dream, the cornerstone of the family, security in tough times, evidence of your labor, and the basis of your wealth. Your home holds your family's treasures, provides shelter against harsh times and realities, and is the source of your legacy to your children.

RELIGION : Attend a church or mosque of your choice. Hang on to your African roots, incorporate them into your chosen course of worship in the new world, and integrate them into your daily routines to teach lessons, ease suffering, relay messages, and confirm the equality of all before God.

RESPECT : Be polite, tell the truth, stay loyal and listen, adopt a moral plan, and learn from your elders; this will be the development of respect for yourself, will guide your respect for others, and will validate the role of family, the place where it all begins. Learn and respect your heritage, the history of your people, and pass it on.

ECONOMIC INDEPENDENCE : Your goal is to amass economic capital through a job or jobs working with your hands and mind for economic independence and a better quality of life. Be sure to set something aside each paycheck for the rainy days. Live within your means and spend wisely. Learn the value of money and the foolishness of overspending.

SOCIAL INTERACTION : It is good to be alone, and solitude can be a beautiful thing. However, the moments you will really remember to the fullest will be those spent with other people. They do not have to be extravagant moments, or out of the ordinary, but simply those moments when the music is right, the companionship is tight, the food and ambiance make you feel like dancing, and this gives rise to collaborative, spontaneous joy.

EDUCATION: Be serious about your studies. Education opens the doors for African Americans and is the one thing that cannot be taken away. It is the pathway to careers, be they professional or skilled. It enables you to have a career and build wealth. Knowledge is power!

HOPE: The day will come when Blackness no longer signals a higher risk than whites of premature death, impoverishment, unemployment, educational gaps, incarceration, victimization, homelessness, and police harassment; all vestiges of racial discrimination will be reduced. You must believe in this or face a life of depression and despair.

MARVIN ROGER ANDERSON, RONDO CENTER OF DIVERSE EXPRESSIONS

RONDO
VALUES

Rondo means family. The foundation of our community is the values that have been passed down from generations of hard-working people.

We are the hope of our ancestors.

I am committed to keeping our community positive. We will achieve this by increasing access to educational obtainment and uplifting our economic status. We will use financial literacy education to teach future generations to invest in real estate

This is how we keep our community strong.

A.T.

I live out the Rondo values by being respectful. I have manners. I'm in student leadership. I'm kind. I go to church with my grandma. I respect others in my community.

LAH'NIYAH CROCKETT

I live out the Rondo values by showing respect because I want people to look at me like I'm a kind kid. I use my manners and kind words. I'm in leadership so the little kids can look up to me. I am respectful.

ZHA'NAIJAH HERRON

I live out the Rondo values by inspiring others to remain hopeful, pursuing higher education, practicing faith daily, and working towards becoming economically independent for the benefit of my family and community. These values make me who I am, and I am proud to have the opportunity to live out these values in the Rondo community.

MAJESTE PHILLIP

I can live out the Rondo values by home ownership. Supporting it and respecting education and religion. And support interaction. I do this at school and home.

CMIYAH

Respect others by being kind and helping and working hard by learning new things and paying attention to important things. Focus on me.

NA'LAH

I can live out the Rondo values at home. Make the world better to stop violence. Stop hurting people. Stop violence. Stop hurting people.

RICKY

I can live out the Rondo values by respecting others' values. Getting education, respecting Rondo and the Rondo community. Respect the people of Rondo and the place. Respect Black women and Black men. Respect all.

CAMDEN

Everybody needs hope, whether it's Rondo, the community people. Who or whatever needs hope, nobody should give up hope. Honestly, it could be the toughest time, but God did not create you to give up now, not ever, because we as a community must give hope to each other, even if we don't know a person. Don't be negative; it is not the best way to go. Choose hope because we are going need it.

JAMIAH WALKER

I like to be outside next to my home, to be close to the things I like about it. There's a park close by, so I like going there to see my friend. I wish I had a cat to pay with outside and when I'm indoors, but I like to read; reading makes me relaxed and calm.

HANA ABDULLAHI

My Rondo elders taught me the importance of family first. My goal is to focus on strengthening families and building hope for the future. The elders also modeled hard work and dedication. The elders promoted social interaction by sharing the wisdom cultivated from their life experiences.

DAVID BUCKHALTON

I like that we can just write. Like as authors. And I like that we can read a lot and get inspired and I can be happy and real calm, and that is things that I like about the Rondo values.

HODAN ABDULLAHI

The biggest, most memorable event of my childhood is Rondo Days. I still remember waking up and running to the intersection of Central and Victoria picking out my spot as I waited for the parade to begin. The best part of the parade was being able to point out relatives, neighbors, and classmates. Watching the parade was like a sneak peek at the drill teams that would be in the dance competition held later that day. Being at that intersection was a time to mingle with some of your favorite people in the neighborhood and see some of the ones you haven't seen since the last parade.

The actual event was usually held at a large park. There'd be food, dancing, singing, shopping, and networking. As an adult attending Rondo Days, you can still get that warm hometown feeling. A place where everyone knows you, or what family you come from. It's like being at a family reunion, or even a high school reunion where it's just good vibes and catching up, and mentally returning to those times when life just felt good.

The Rondo Neighborhood was always my safe place. I was thankful enough to be raised my whole childhood there. I had an aunt, uncle, grandma, blood cousins, play cousins, and lifelong friends who were part of the community then and now. I loved walking, walking, walking, to the left you'd get to Dairy Queen, to the right you'd get to Wendy's. I remember riding my bike across the bridge that separated the neighborhood, overlooking the freeway. On that same bridge, I would jump every time a car passed underneath, these were good times.

The Rondo Neighborhood is where I mimicked things that I saw and learned to push myself harder if things didn't look right. This is the place where I went to church and saw businesses right in the neighborhood owned and run by people who looked like me. This is the place where I saw many homeowners who also looked like me. They raised their children and kept going no matter what obstacles appeared. So many things to say about Rondo, and even now that my journey has taken me outside of the community, when I come home because it will always be my home, I always FEEL it.

LATAI FEARSON

The Rondo neighborhood was shaped by the foundation of community. This allowed emphasis on the Rondo values to ensure that the community would remain for generations to come.

There was an understanding and realization that to obtain economic and social connection for African Americans, these core principles would sustain the well-being and growth of the Rondo neighborhood.

As a member of this community since the age of thirteen, I continue to reside in the Rondo neighborhood and live out these values. This is evident in the book I wrote for the St. Paul Public Schools, titled *We Can Learn Together*, as well as presentations to students in the St. Paul Public School District. Artwork that I created also adorns the walls of the Rondo Library.

Critical to community well-being is spirituality. Religion and faith serve as a vehicle for a moral compass and advocacy to improve the lives of those in the community. I have painted murals for two churches in the Rondo community. I am the president of the Central Village Homeowners Association. I have served in this role since 2008. In addition, I have been a member of the District 8 Planning Council. These are more than just positions. It is the ability to ensure that we keep a sense of community and maintain a place that is a nucleus for one's sense of self, connection, and growth.

DONALD WALKER

The mind and spirit of the warrior is stalwart, resolved, unwavering, unbending, and uncompromising when it comes to justice. Therefore, the warrior sees, hears, feels, and responds to injustice in a matter that is clear and resolute. It is both relevant and timely to speak the story of Black Rondo with the voice of the warrior, as there have been recent events in the region that have resurrected the zeitgeist of warriorhood among American Descendants of Slaves.

THE ARCHITECT

I live out the Rondo values by participating in the Rondo parade and bringing my children, grandchildren, friends, and organizations. Also, I come to activities at Rondo Library. Here is Rondo community and I hope it continues to grow.

GLORIA LITTLE

I grew up in Rondo learning so many things. I always hung out at the Jimmy Lee Center, getting paid to take educational classes, learning about my body, the person I can grow up to be. So I always live out Rondo's education values by showing what I've learned.

MYISHA FARMER

Social interaction is a great way for me to keep the core values of our community together. I love our close-knit community we have in our Rondo Village.

SERISA CRYER

Our core family value is social interaction. Rondo is a resilient community made up of African Americans who migrated from different areas of the South.

Their goal was to start a new life which was nurtured by new friendships, and that blossomed into kinship networks.

JACKLYN MILTON

Sometimes I am the eyes and ears of the Rondo community. When I sit in a meeting and people are talking about the dismantlement of I-94, they don't know who is in their audience.

Management explains they don't want to make the same mistakes as they did with I-94 when they did not involve the Rondo community. This is when I must tell them I am that little Rondo girl whose community was destroyed, who experienced the effects of a dismantled I-94 with other people in the community.

Until you walk in our shoes, your life is disrupted, and the business you work for has been destroyed, you will not understand our Rondo history. That is a hurt sometimes you may never recover from, or you may not get a second chance because of who you are.

My place of employment is the Minnesota Department of Transportation (MnDOT).

What did it do to our community? Who am I? I am the daughter of Jinnie B. (Land) and John Cauley. The sister of Jeanette Adams (Jeanette Avaloz) and Kevin Cauley, and the granddaughter of Mary Clupper. My name is Shalette Cauley (Cauley-Wandrick), the little girl who grew in the community and still remembers Rondo.

SHALETTE CAULEY-WANDRICK

A CALL TO LEADERSHIP

A leader is one who sets a good example for others to see and emulate if they also wish to strengthen the Rondo community. Setting a good example means that the leader is willing to listen attentively, tolerate mistakes, recognize the potential in others, communicate honestly, and gives others credit for their ideas and suggestions.

Leadership requires the setting of goals and expectations yet understands that flexibility is necessary under certain conditions. Any one of the attributes above could serve as the "one leadership action" to strengthen Rondo. But, these listings can also function as adjectives for the number one leadership quality not listed: collaborate.

There's an old saying: If you want to go fast, go alone; if you want to go far, go with a group. While some may wish there was "the one" to lead the return of Rondo, the wise will understand that it will be a group working together, setting good examples, recognizing the potential in others, etc. that will eventually get us where we need to go as a community.

MARVIN ROGER ANDERSON

Music as a Great Healer

Since coming to St. Paul, MN in 1958, I have always been immersed in the beauty of the Rondo Community, a very special community of people who love and share so many beautiful ideas. It's a place where you really get to know your neighbors.

Having to move out of the community because of the freeway being built, I felt I had lost the school that my sons attended. Some of my favorite spots were torn down, like Art's Barber shop, small stores on the corners of our neighborhood, the pharmacy on Rondo.

People had to leave, like Hallie Q. Brown and so many others that lived on my street. We attended the neighborhood churches, which included Mt. Olivet, where I served as Minister of Music for over 20 years. I am still in the Rondo Community, where we were partners to a new church and a senior building. I was also the co-founder of Walker West Music Academy since 1988, and am presently expanding our presence with people from all over the Twin Cities and beyond.

For leadership action going forward, continue to bring the community together, offering music as a great healer in our community and also as a connector for others who are new to our wonderful community.

REV. CARL WALKER

Black Rondo: They killed our mother, and we didn't have time to weep when she died!

Black Rondo was our mother. She was killed, and we didn't have time to weep when she died. We (the children of Black Rondo) were too busy trying to survive! But in our fight for survival, we have not forgotten the burden paid, lessons taught, nor vision of our mother. Oh (Mo'dear) Black Rondo, you gave birth to our hopes, to our humanity, to our independence, to our health, and to our dignity. We are your children and your power, presence, essence, and your spirit will forever live in us and through our work to honor your memory.

WITH LOVE, YOUR BLACK BABIES OF RONDO!

It is in this very moment some of you think you just heard another retelling of the story of Rondo. If this is what you believe, then you have misunderstood every word that was conveyed.

For the warrior is not an intellectual, nor a businessman, nor a politician. Neither is the warrior a griot of the community. The warrior does not retell the history of their people. The warrior reclaims! In the name of the Most High whose hands have fashioned our souls, we the (warriors) "children of Black Rondo" are reclaiming all that was taken from us. And we live by the warrior oath, "Freedom or death!"

We are reclaiming that which was taken by force, by coercion, by abusive policies, by intimidation, by deceit, and by other acts of political and economic skullduggery. We will not deviate from our course. Our hearts are full, our minds sharp, our bodies tested, and our spirits resolved.

The children of Black Rondo have steadied our hands for battle, and in this fight for justice, humanity, full personhood, and unequivocal reparation we will stop at nothing short of victory.

WE MUST WIN!

We must win our right to proper education, our right to non-abusive relationships, our right to adequate healthcare, our right to ownership, our right to appropriate employment, our right to autonomy, our right to full personhood, and our right to self-governance!

We are responding to the declaration of war on our lives, and we will engage in strategic battle as "unified pawns" until the victory is won! Now let the community and ancestors respond as one in saying, "Ase!"

THE ARCHITECT

I would help the Rondo community through giving them hope. Hope for a better future, for education so kids like me can feel safe and accomplished. And I would help others give hope for respecting people of all colors and religions. And even more hope will help our community to be strong, safe, respectful, and it would feel like home.

HAWA FARAH

Helping organize community events within the Rondo Community.
Volunteer at schools within the Rondo Community.

NYIA HARRIS

Rondo community as an inner-city big family, provide more connections to people. Be more connected as the people living in the suburbs. We need to love Rondo, protect it, and support it. Go, Rondo!!!

SOPHIE LIU-OTHMER

Connect kids in the community to college and provide support for them throughout their education. Connect high school students and college students to internships. Bring resources from around the region and even across the country of the community to help kids pursue education.

YANMEI JIANG

One leadership action I have participated in is public policy work for affordable housing work with the County Commissioner, City Council, and the people in the community. Also by attending church at Camphor Memorial United Methodist Church.

GLORIA LITTLE

Home ownership is the way I give back to our Rondo community. We need to have a piece of the pie for our overall growth to continue for generations to come.

SERISA CRYER

I can strengthen the Rondo community by showing people respect and fighting for my rights and for every other Black person. I do this by standing up for myself and telling people about my amazing culture. I am also going to be respectful and kind by showing respect to others, like being kind, helpful, and caring.

RA'MYJAH BUMPUS

I can strengthen the Rondo community by doing my best, working hard, helping you do the best you can every day. Everybody can do it; you can do it. Respect others. For example, if you see someone not doing their best, say, "Hey, try your best to do your best." It's never over.

CAMDEN MORGAN

Leadership actions I can take to strengthen the Rondo community are to fight for equal rights, STOP racism, help whenever I can—and by doing. That is how I can strengthen the Rondo community. The sky's the limit when you believe.

CORNELIUS SANGSTER, JR.

I can strengthen the Rondo community by going to school and helping. I will help the community by cleaning up, including others, and not judging or making fun of people.

DEARIEA COLLINS

I strengthen the Rondo community by showing empathy. I can show empathy by being kind, honest, and respectful, by helping others, being selfless, and caring for others. I would also show empathy by respecting people's culture and what they believe.

NA'LAH JENNINGS

One leadership action that I can take is to be a safe keeper of Rondo's story by sharing it with those within my local community. Leadership demands that we support one another. A great way to support one another is to remind ourselves that we are the products of strong communities like Rondo. Every time we tell the stories of Rondo, we keep its shared history alive in ways that allow us to foster its spirit in our own communities today.

I live out the Rondo values by being a meaningful part of my community. The spirit of Rondo consists of a tight-knit group of people, having a shared interest in being cooperative with one another to each other's benefit for no reason other than embracing love. It means a lot to me to have a number of people that I can count on to support and uplift me; it brings me joy to know that they have the same in me.

The values of social interaction and education speak to my community impact strongly. I make it a point to physically show up for my community members and ensure that fellowship happens in follow-up. Each moment of time shared creates an opportunity to maintain a connection of support thereafter. When it comes to education, I spend my free time supporting the literacy of children to create learning opportunities outside of the classroom. As a member of my community, and as someone who privileges maintaining the history and values of Rondo, I believe it is my duty to support youth in actualizing their own leadership skills. It takes a village to raise a child, but it also takes this same village to support that child through adulthood.

NGERI AZUEWAH

Work- I live out Rondo's values in my work by showing up and seeing what ways we as Black people can advance. I work to remove barriers and unfair practices by calling them out. I work to create mentorship and leadership development opportunities for the community. I am constantly working towards change.

Homeownership- I live out my homeownership value by preparing myself to become a homeowner. I connect with organizations that support home ownership and build knowledge of the processes that can interfere with homeownership.

I also lead homeowner & renters justice forums to bring resources to the community.

Religion- I live out religion by studying my bible, showing up at my church, and giving back to the community.

Respect- We are all here. We work better when our work is supported. We can then reach those who are lost.

Economic Independence- I am learning how the community works and sharing what I learn. I am connecting with community partners to learn how to become financially stable and build generational wealth.

Social Interaction- I am working together with others and building our Black communities. I am working to change the lens through which some of us value or devalue ourselves. No longer will we let others tell our truth.

Education- I am empowering our future generations by building literacy & reading comprehension skills and boosting the confidence needed to take action.

Hope- We got this. God first and the rest will fall into place regardless of who tries to interfere.

UNIQUE TRIPP

REFLECTION GUIDE

These writing prompts can serve as a guide for learning more about your cultural heritage and roots. Gather a group of students, friends, and family members to pause, reflect, and grow.

Reflection Questions

What is the history of Rondo? How was it impacted by the 1956 Federal Interstate Highway Act and the construction of I-94? Were other Black communities impacted by the highway system in your state?

What are the core values of Rondo?

How do you live out your family and community values?

What is one leadership action you can take to strengthen your community?

ABOUT THE ARTIST

Broderick Poole

Broderick Poole is a Rondo-based visual artist who specializes in creating multiple forms of custom handcrafted art. He's been creating artwork for over twenty-five years and for the past several years has been teaching the youth in the neighborhood he grew up in.

www.ingramcontent.com/pod-product-compliance
Lightning Source LLC
Chambersburg PA
CBHW060807090426
42736CB00002B/182